Europe:
A Mission
Misunderstood

Eddy Duru

authorHOUSE®

AuthorHouse™ UK Ltd.
500 Avebury Boulevard
Central Milton Keynes, MK9 2BE
www.authorhouse.co.uk
Phone: 08001974150

First published by AuthorHouse 9/13/2010

ISBN: 978-1-4520-7703-1 (sc)

Dedication

This book is dedicated to my beloved son Marvin Kelechi Komi Duru and all the other children born in the course of this struggle.

Acknowledgement

I would love to give big thanks to my greatest companion, Lord and Master Jesus Christ, whose grace I have enjoyed so much. Everything I am and all I will be is all because of him. He never loses any battle. Take glory, Father, Son, and the Holy Spirit.

To my grandmother of blessed memory, Nne Ukwu, whose love never left me, I say thank you.

Thanks to my wonderful daddy, Prince E. E. Duruh, and Mum, who trained me. Your training and understanding are never to be forgotten, and to the whole of Eluchie Duruh's family, I say thank you.

I remember when I was elected the "catholic youths" president in my parish years ago; I thought you were going to be mad at me for accepting such a time-demanding position considering my academic pursuits and my commitment to our company. Instead, you welcomed it with joy, saying that as long as it is God's service, I was free to go ahead with the post.

That leadership position has been a great part of my foundation.

To the youth members of Holy Spirit Catholic Church parish of Benin City, I thank you all for the opportunity to serve. It was truly a training ground. Thanks to my son, Marvin Kelechi Komi Duru, whose time I sometimes took to fight even the course of others and his mother too.

My gratitude to my wife, Ijeoma L. Duru, whose friendship and encouragement cannot be measured. My thanks goes to the members of Igbo union, and other unions in Kassel for their brotherly love.

Thanks to Jonas, who has been a faithful brother to me since I met him.

I acknowledge the Green & More team for your service and contributions. Thanks also to Mr. Stephen Amenyo, Reverend. Father Donatus Onuigbo and Mr. Celestine Odo for your wonderful contributions.

My gratitude goes to Pastor Daniel Asamoah for all his prayer support. I acknowledge with thanks my friends and colleagues Frank Okey Collins and Lewis Ehiwario, who have been part of this struggle in a special way.

And to all African leaders and friends in Europe who have made one contribution or another, space will not permit me to mention your names one by one, but I say more grease to your elbows. I appreciate your commitment to serving our people.

Contents

Introduction   11

Chapter   1 How It All Started   13

Chapter 2 The Black Man I Know   17

Chapter 3 Thoughts and Plans   22

Chapter 4 Welcome to Germany/ Europe   25

Chapter 5 Fear, Frustration, and Depression   34

Chapter 6 Crime   45

Chapter 7 Marriage and Kids   48

Chapter 8 The Worth of Man   57

Chapter 9 Discrimination   65

Chapter 10 The Real Man   73

Chapter 11 Time to Rethink   81

About the Author   87

Introduction

Wealth, riches, happiness, successes, joy, breakthroughs, luck, championship, poverty, and even failures are part of our existence and will continue to be, irrespective of who we are and where we exist.

This book may change the course of your thinking about life in general. It will cause you to look at both success and failure in the right way, thereby allowing you to make the best out of every situation in life.

The stories contained in this book are true. I have been a living witness to them and I am still trying to answer my questions and those of many others.

It was not my intention to mention people's names and data in this book. But I would plead with all who may be affected in any way to bear with me and to know that as it applies to one, so it applies to most.

For many, the idea of the journey was defeated as soon as they entered the airplane to the life unknown.

You can make it anywhere if you have the right direction; it's just that we lacked the necessary information, patience, courage, and truth.

This book attempts to reveal the truth, as the Bible teaches us that we shall know the truth and it shall set us free.

Success means different things to different people; true success, however, means more than just one break-through.

This book tries to define **who we are, where we are coming from, and the status of the current European society. It also explores how far we have come, what hope the future holds for us, how we need to rethink, and much more**.

It is my aim to make this book simple and straight forward for the understanding of all classes of readers so as to present an easier research work and debate that will produce a better personal life result.

Get the experienced knowledge and truth and may the spirit of God lead us into making and achieving the best results.

Chapter 1

How It All Started

Africa, where I come from, is a continent made up of different countries and people with different social profiles.

Some of these countries are devastated by war and overwhelmed with hopelessness. Some have no physical war but are experiencing very terrible cold wars. Some are ruled by military juntas who coercively took over the realm of power without recourse to the rule of law.

Some of these countries such as Nigeria, are very rich and endowed with enormous natural resources. But regrettably, the leaders and also some of the citizens are profoundly corrupt. Some African families are so poor that they cannot afford a day's meals, let alone think of sending their kids to school. Some families are able to afford three square meals a day, send their kids to school, plan their futures and even maintain a home.

It is, however, surprising to affirm that some Africans are so rich that even their dogs grow bigger than lions. But the numbers of these people are few and they could afford to be in different places at different times, just on demand because the money is there.

The educational system (Bildungssystem) in Nigeria is very different from the German system. While Germans invest much in their training institutions and universities, Nigerians seems to pay more attention to university levels. After nursery school, which takes three years, one moves to primary school to spend six years, after which one is eligible to enrol in a secondary school, but only if one's common entrance exam is successful.

Secondary education in Nigeria is divided into two levels, the junior secondary school lasting for three years and the senior secondary, which takes another three years, making it a total of six years combined. At the end of the secondary education, which is considered part of standard education in Nigeria, some will proceed to the university or other institutions of higher learning if their families can afford it, while others move to other walks of life.

Meanwhile, for different reasons, there are people who never acquire formal education. The Nigerian system does not offer free education even though it has the financial capability to do so.

We also have apprentices who spend between three and eight years with their masters after which they are expected to be settled depending on the type of agreement signed. This is another system of educational training though with little or no academic attachment.

Both the academic groups, business ones and traders, could be successful in Nigeria if the system were better organised.

But the corruption and greed that started from the top and made their way to the ordinary man have made it so difficult, and almost impossible, for many to earn a living.

So if you can't beat them, you join them, as they say. What a pity!

With particular reference to my country of origin, Nigeria, it used to be a sweet lovely country in the late 1970s up to the early 1980s. During this period, the naira which is the national currency was even more valuable than the US dollar and German mark. People who travelled to the USA and Europe in the 1970s and 1980s did so only to acquire academic and technological knowledge, coming back after their studies to contribute meaningfully to the growth of our beloved country.

But staying in Nigeria was also great, and the young men and women had no reason to travel. Corruption had not reached the level it is at today. But when the military took over power, the situation in the country worsened. There was no rule of law, no freedom of speech, no freedom of the press, no freedom of association, no respect for the constitution, and no respect for judicial verdicts. The whole system was broken down and corruption rose to the maximum. Leaders turned self-centred and personal accumulation of national wealth became the order. Killing and jailing without judicial trial became the order of the day. Nobody dared challenge the military dictatorship as grave consequences awaited anybody or group who acted otherwise.

Human rights were seriously abused and corruption rose to the maximum.

Natural resources that could serve the needs of every Nigerian became sources of funds for perpetuating parochial interests by the ruling military juntas and their cronies. The masses were left to suffer, thereby encouraging crimes and modern slavery. Academic pursuit and qualitative learning were discouraged. Schools and universities were sometimes closed down for several months. Teachers and lecturers were not paid, although more natural resources continued to be discovered.

Since the late 1990s, democracy has been partially restored through civil rule but the rudiments of democracy are still far from being realised. The greed and corruption, that eat so deep into the minds and hearts of the leaders and many other citizens remains a chronic issue.

Chapter 2

The Black Man I Know

Classisification of people, race, or community, depends on the behaviour of such people. If the average population of a community behave similar, such behaviour could be attributed to them. This also does not mean that people always behave alike. There are always exceptions. There are both good and bad people everywhere but this book tries to define the average black man.

A black man would not want to die for anyone or anything. He loves his life so much and would try hard to preserve it. He would probably not risk his life in any form of research or experimental programme. He is fearful and tries to avoid trouble. He loves and enjoys good living, but that often remain a dream. Other factors attributable to a black man are envy and backbiting, which makes him unnecessarily interfere with other people's issue that have nothing to do with him. In addition, he would like to work fewer hours but make more money in order to enjoy himself and keep up with his numerous needs.

The black race has the culture of an extended family system, which sometimes makes it difficult to define some family relationships, but which gives joy in most cases.

Religion which was brought to us by the white man has long been overtaken by the black man. Though a black man may not be destructively fanatic about religion, I can tell you that a lot could die for the sake of religious beliefs if you want to kill them. If you give a black man a million dollars to go and practice suicide bombing, he would welcome the monetary offer with great joy, but he would do everything possible to run away with your money without dying or killing anyone. No mater how hard it looks, a black man would not commit suicide; he would always want to continue trying. He loves his live too much to give it up.

An African man believes in God and trusts in Jesus. It is a normal family tradition to worship Jehovah God. Going to church every Sunday must be observed, as tradition demands, and through such healthy tradition, many have been born again in Christ Jesus. Places of worship are scattered all over the place more than one can find Sparkasse Bank in Germany. Traditional values are also not neglected even though Christianity seems to over power the whole traditional values these days.

There is no region of the world without crime and the average black man is not crime minded. Some were forced by poverty to indulge in criminal activities in the past. Drugs like cocaine, heroin, and marijuana are like taboo to the ears of many. They are hardly seen and people who even mention such names are often discriminated against in the society. An average African with a religious family background knew little or nothing about hard drugs and wanted nothing to do with them. Being in the house of God every Sunday and sometimes weekdays is a tradition, and he or she always has in mind that the more one goes to school, the more one learns. So in Christianity, the more you hear the gospel preached, the more you develop the fear, trust and love for God.

Many got closer to God to the extent that they could even abandoned their lives to follow Jesus. Commitment to God is in no way strange to the ears of these people, even the very old who were formerly traditional worshippers. They believed in him and his ultimate power. The black man I know may have an instinct for greed and such a negative trait could perhaps be attributed to the African extended family system. It may also be attributed to ignorance or lack of knowledge. I call it poverty of the brain. For instance, if well managed, Nigeria is capable of paying social security to her citizens and even providing adequate infrastructures for the rapid development of the country.

If those African leaders who travel around the world to see how it is over there, get US and EU medical treatment, could still be so greedy as to hide our money in the outside world, leaving the immediate world around them to suffer and die in poverty, how then could one describe such an ugly situation? Sickness and poverty of the brain! Not just greediness. It's obviously worst than that.

I recently travelled to Abuja in Nigeria, after being informed of how beautiful the city is. I saw that the city was beautifully built. But if one moved outside Abuja towards the eastern part of Nigeria, one would begin to see and feel frustration everywhere, on the roads, all over people's faces, even in the air. Given such, one questions, why other states can't be like Abuja or something close to it? The answer is simply sickness or poverty of the brain associated not only with our leaders but also with other masses that surely need the re-education that this book is trying to offer.

There are people living in mansions with large compounds fenced as high as national stadiums but they do not have roads to enter such mansions. Some people have standby electric generators and even discourage regular power supply in order to boom generator, gas, and oil businesses.

There is mass exodus of African youths to Europe and other foreign countries today, and our leaders and foreign extractors are not free of the blame. **But every individual still remains responsible for every decision he or she makes.**

Remember that most African countries are richly blessed with natural resources and all we need are proper management, sound mind, healthy brain, selflessness, contentment, and commitment. I've never met anybody from Saudi Arabia, Kuwait, the United Arab-Emirates and many other countries also blessed with natural resources, who was seeking asylum in Europe the way we do. It's all about commitment and good governance.

Chapter 3

Thoughts and Plans

In the midst of riches, poverty, sufferings, successes, pride, oppression, war, lies, freedom, abuses, communication, information and misinformation, diverse thoughts were born in the hearts of people. Thoughts of travelling to Europe, the so-called green pasture, started to arise. One of my course mates at the university always had some US dollars and German marks in his wallet. He'd already concluded that he was going to end up in any of the G8 countries even though we had not yet graduated. He travelled to Europe, got deported and having experienced both sides, swore never to travel there again.

Another person, a business man, who had four boys working under him, thought he would travel to Europe, work for two years to make some money to add to his business and go back to his business and family. But he ended up spending a year and half in jail, because of lies and wrong information before his journey in Europe even started.

Several people who travelled for economic reasons, never planned to stay longer than three years, but at the end of the day, they either ended up just living without any plan, or possibly taking their lives for those who could no longer carry on. Travelling to Europe must be well planned. Irrespective of one's present situation one must ask himself several questions and possibly answer them all before setting off on the journey. Ask yourself this question: Do I want to join a foreign world that probably has little or nothing to do with me, my world, my culture, my race, my system, my belief, my values and so on? Then find out first who you are, what you can do, what you want, what God wants from you and why you must live your world.

Remember you are about to make a personal life decision. I heard some say they were travelling to Europe to make money after which their world would turn around for the better. Some dreamt of marrying and living with white women. Others thought they could have their peace in Europe. Some people left Africa because of insecurity, hoping to enjoy the supposedly security, joy, peace, and tranquillity that Europe offers only to be disappointed.

Germany is a great country. It was built from few natural resources to a super power by selfless, committed, and sound minded people who were interested in their people. They made good use of their man-power, technology and research. Yes. Germany and Germans are great! But is that your world?

I'm not suggesting that Africa and Nigeria have become better and stronger than Germany now. But with what we Nigerians have, such as, our natural resources, we could be more similar to Germany, if not become stronger.

Chapter 4

Welcome to Germany/ Europe

For many people, the journey to Europe ends as soon as they entered the aircraft to the world unknown. The image our people in Europe present to those at home, even at the airport, makes the situation even worse. Some fake agents who prepare travel documents but never travel themselves, deceive lots of people who end up getting more frustrated than ever.

I remember the great zeal I had when I first entered Germany, thinking of how I was going to further my studies and also invest all my man power in working in order to make life worth living. After going through the whole frustrating and intimidating process of trying to stay, I was finally posted to Baunatal in Kassel.

Without wasting any more time after being posted from one place to the other, I started looking for work immediately, thinking that that is how it worked here. Every morning when I woke up, I would pray, carry my bag with some food and drink and start going from one company to the other in search of work. Each place I went, I was asked for my work permit, which I could not produce, and asked what type of residence permit I had. One of the companies in Kassel's industrial layout later offered to give me a job after sympathising with me, but on a condition that I get a work permit from the Ministry of Works.

I asked the company to give me an employment confirmation to aid me in getting the work permit from the work ministry. They did give me the confirmation, which I took with me to Ministry of Works.

The work ministry reminded me that I could not get a work permit as long as I was seeking asylum and not yet married. I was also reminded of different categories of people when it came to job offers: the German citizens, Europeans, those married to Germans, and several other categories bringing me to the last category then.

I was highly demoralised and frustrated. But I did not forget that all are created equal and no human is illegal. Well that is the law!

A friend from Dusseldorf, whom I met at the Nigerian embassy in Berlin told me a story about one of his friends who'd recently jumped into a running water canal after spending several years in Germany.

Another friend of his was sent some money by his parents to enable him to return home. People tried to put smile on their faces but they would rather die.

Hardly anyone you meet doesn't have a shocking story to tell. Constant rise of blood pressure and growing grey hairs became common to most young ones. The big issue remains: which way out? For many, it's a life of constant fear and tension; shock at every little noise becomes some people's ways of life. Some get so confused and miserable that even if you paid for their flight ticket, they wouldn't go home. Their argument remains: Where would they go after several years in Europe? With whom and where would they start from when they got home? Some no longer had homes, no families, no cars and no money while the people they left years earlier had re- established in different ways, having stable families and means of livelihood. They were people giving out fake smiles although they were almost dead inside.

One immigrant who was to face deportation, and he fought so hard with the authorities to avoid being deported. Unfortunately, he attempted suicide afterwards. He was brought back back to jail, where he underwent some psychiatric treatment. As I visited him in the jail for an interview, he poured out his heart to me, telling me how he's been in Germany for twelve years. Before he travelled, he was a successful trader with a fiancée who loved him so much.

A year before he started nursing the idea of travelling to Europe, he had ordered some goods from China, thereby, establishing an Asian contact. Shortly afterwards, he discussed with his parents whether they could sell their house in the big city to support his steadily bumming business. His loving parents sold the house and gave him the money.

After he got the money, one of his friends who lived in Germany came back home after seven years. He returned with six used cars and was processing the papers for clearing the cars from the seaport. While the trader had just one car, he also had a home of his own, a woman he loved, his steadily growing business, the new Asian contact he's made, and his caring and loving parents, who were always ready to support him. His environment, his_people, his world. Hanging out with his German friend who shipped six used cars, he asked him how he made it in seven years. The idea of six cars was very heart-warming. In fact, in discussing it with his friend, he decided to travel to Germany, with the notion that if his friend, who he didn't consider as smart as himself could make it in seven years, he could make it in two years. And possibly buy a bigger house than the one his parents had sold to support his business.

So there he went! After selling everything he had, he followed his friend to Germany. His fiancée never knew what was going on until the travel arrangements were almost concluded. When she learned of what he was doing, she frowned at the idea since her husband-to-be was already doing well. But the guy couldn't get over the fact that his friend had brought in six cars in seven years.

He promised his fiancée he'd return within two years. He even came to Germany with 2,700DM which was later taken away from him because he identified himself falsely. That was his first shock at the airport in Germany. When they'd arrived at the airport, they'd passed through the immigration formality, and he was happy. But his friend went up to get a taxi to take them to the train station, and he told him to wait behind, having collected his travel documents that he prepared for him. While he was waiting for his friend, who was also careful not to be identified with him, he got controlled at the airport and his friend disappeared immediately.

Meanwhile, on their flight, his friend had already prepared him for such emergencies as police control.

He could not identify himself well and his purpose of travel could not be proved. In the midst of that shock after much interrogation, he declared himself a political refugee. He spent six days at the airport jail, living only on bread and tea after which he was taken to a refugee camp. Telling his story, he was granted temporary political asylum. Later, after spending seven months in the asylum camp, he was posted to a permanent Asylum home in the eastern part of Germany.

While in that concentrated asylum home, he had to get permission to come and go, which is likened to high school students in a fenced school hostel with security. Cooked foods were served according to the authorities' time table. If one missed his or her food ration, the person would not only go hungry but may also be penalised. Every movement required permission. Apart from suffering from running stomach due to the change in diet, it was also a wasted seven to eight months of brain torture, according to him. All he did was sleep, eat, watch the ceiling, think and then sleep again.

One is not even allowed to sleep overnight outside the camp unless permission is sought and obtained. In addition, one is not permitted to engage in any kind of job. As a refugee, one is kept and fed in a place.

When he was finally posted to a permanent place, he thought that his journey had started, but he was only to be confronted with a new form of war, which is the war of letters. Germans believe in writing and keeping documents. To every issue, big or small, there is always a letter to back it up. Constant visits to lawyers became part of his daily business. He was paired in a room with a dirty guy who turned alcoholic even before the final transfer. He fought to be removed from the room, but to no avail. Remember, he came to look for money, and with his state of mind, he needed some peace and tranquillity. But the problem of him being paired in a room with an alcoholic worried him more.

The house master and the social workers were introduced to him. The transportation system was also introduced and explained to him, whereby he had to trek some kilometres to get to a bus station: otherwise he has to wait for two hours. And after six o'clock, he had to walk home if he happened to be somewhere in the city because the bus that went to his area stopped running at six. He was allowed to cook for himself now but with precaution.

He received *schein* on a weekly basis, allowing him to go to a specified shop to collect foodstuffs for cooking. If he failed to collect his food *schein* for one week, he would go hungry. In addition, he may be questioned for failing to collect it.

With regards to money, he received eighty-one deutsche mark every month as pocket money, with which he got around, paid his lawyer, and took care of other things. He had to cook the kind of food imposed on him since he couldn't afford the African foodstuff he was used to. He had been restricted to a certain local government area and was not allowed to cross his local boundaries without a genuine permission from the alien authorities in his local area. These are other forms of brain torture!

For ten years, he lived that way. He was almost hopeless. Letters continued filling his letter box for many reasons. For instance, he has no freedom, no working permit, and the money he brought has gone his real identity still unknown to the authorities. He declared his loving parents dead in order to make a case. He also denied his beloved fiancée, while time continued running. He kept consulting one lawyer after another looking for a solution to his problem.

He was taken from one embassy to another by the authorities, who were trying to figure out exactly where he came from in other to deport him back. His life was agony, his world crumbled.

He made an acquaintance sometime who took him to an asylum house somewhere in Hamburg. In fact, he decided to join the guy without asking for any permission after the guy told him how much easier it was there only to meet another group of people he believed was far better off.

These were people who had given up hope. He met mostly blacks who always fed on marijuana; he'd never even seen marijuana while he was in Africa. But there in Hamburg, it was like food without season. He was even forced to smoke; otherwise they would not assist him in any way. A fight occurred one day in the Hamburg asylum home, and then there was police control there. He was sent back to his own asylum home and had to pay a fine for leaving his local area to another without permission.

The whole situation lasted for ten years before the issue of his deportation got intensified again. In fact, he was to be deported to any African country since his real identity was unknown.

I quickly asked him why his friend didn't tell him the truth about life in Europe and what his friend exactly did in Germany. He responded that his friend told him that Germany was not easy, but he did not go into details.

More pathetic was that he had a baby with a German woman, who vowed never to let him have custody of his child.

Remember that this discussion/interview was carried out in jail, where he was still awaiting deportation and receiving some psychiatric treatment.

For the past two years, he had lost contact with his fiancée, and he believes she is tired of waiting. He said to me, "Eddy, I have lost everything. I wish I could turn back the hands of time. For now, there is neither beginning nor end. My life, my fiancée, my business, my world... are all in shamble, he wept. "Do something to save me before it's too late." I shed tears with him too but with my face down to avoid making him lose courage. Judge this young man's life story yourself, you who are still planning to sell-off your existence in order to travel to Europe.

Chapter 5

Fear, Frustration, and Depression

I overheard her scream as she was declared a psychiatric patient and was encouraged by her doctor to enter a psychiatric home. "I know my problem! I know my problem! I'm not mad!" she announced. "But I don't know how to solve it. God, do you still exist?" she questioned. "*Deutschland has made me kaput!*" she screamed. "*Ich hasse mein leben, ich hasse euch alle!*" I hate my life: I hate you all! She had visited many doctors and hospitals without finding a solution. She had inflicted injury on herself several times while trying to take her life. She suddenly turned hostile to herself and the world around her. Crying and being in a bad mood became part of her life. She used to be an angelic, lovely, good-looking young girl.

I started feeling guilty even though I was not responsible for her coming to Germany. I even went as far as taking her to the city's mayor, but the outcome was rather shocking. This was the same mayor that came to my house with regards to his election campaign, and I did contribute to his victory, but he could not even help the situation. This shows how critical it could be here. She had left her world in Asia to Germany for personal reasons. While in Asia, as an only daughter, she had two brothers and her late father was a pilot who treated her like a queen while he was alive.

After her father died in an explosion she said they became fearful and insecure in their environment. As they tried to find out the cause of the explosion, their lives became more endangered, which also resulted in some kind of psychological trauma. They finally decided to move to Germany, hoping to enjoy the tranquillity that Europe supposedly offers. However, rather than getting closer to a solution, she became lost touch with the reality of life. The world of illusion took over. The psychiatric bills would be taken care of, but nobody is ever healed when the real issue is not addressed. She said that she had no paper, no work, no future, no freedom, and no money. She once made a trip to Hamburg to her aunt, who wanted her to come for a visit. She travelled to Hamburg without permission from the foreign office believing that she would not be permitted. She unfortunately got controlled by the police at the Hamburg main train station and was immediately sent back to her station without seeing her aunt. She cried that day, she said, and got even more frustrated. In fact, she was almost helpless because there was no plan in sight and no rest. Each day that passed without a letter in her letter box became a great day for her. She even sometimes talks to herself. To her, Germany became a sickness instead of a solution.

I was even encouraged to marry her in other to make her stay, but was that a good solution to her problem? I think not.

Because of parental training in hometowns and Big Brother's restrictions in the city, many children were never allowed to just be teenagers. The problems do not end there. They continue from asylum homes to refugee camps in Europe to police and foreign office control. Such problems will drive a male to a German woman, making him papa. Unfortunately, before you know it, life that never began, ends up just like that.

For many, it was to be a short journey of two to three years, just to work hard, make some money, and go back home. Many left their families, their wives and kids. Some sold off their means of livelihood, such as their businesses, not to mention their family homes and cars. Some even gave up their education and careers just to travel to Europe, thereby abandoning their cultural values only to join this world of illusion. It goes with the saying that, the more you look, the less you see.

Without knowing the consequences of such declaration, an acquaintance of mine willingly allowed himself to be registered as a mentally retarded person by the authorities in Germany. He did it in order to be considered a lunatic, enabling him stay in Germany. He recently got to know the official damage he'd done to himself after I explained the consequences of such a declaration to him now that he's gotten the so-called paper. A mentally retarded person is restricted and cannot do everything. For instance, some type of job employment may not be offered to such a person, and he may not even attain permission to become self-employed. Everyone trying to develop his or her own trick in other to stay in Europe, not minding the damage it could cause. People are tired, downcast, worn out, dismayed, and depressed, but most times, they cry to the wrong people. These mountains of problems have made the youths start growing gray hairs in foreign lands due to frustration.

The sudden deportation of a boy who did his school practical's in my company raised outburst in my city lately. I was also a bit surprised because that was the fastest deportation I had ever witnessed in Germany. When I turned on my mobile telephone that morning, I saw several missed calls and messages from the deported victim and people that lived with him. Before I could rush out to see what I could do for him, he was already at the airport to board the next flight to Africa.

He had come to Germany some five years ago for reasons best known to him. His asylum case was rejected, but he was still allowed to go to school since he was under 18 years. After completing his school and industrial attachment, the authorities had him first look for a job before he could receive permission to work. He got a job and went back to the authorities to ask for work permission. He was told to wait for a while, only to be separated suddenly from his beloved girl friend that early fateful morning. The young boy was suddenly destabilised as far as all his future plans. Only God knows the shock and trauma that boy went through.

The issue of fear and frustration cannot be over emphasised. A state prosecutor once told me in a court yard during break time that he had only met three blacks, he considers responsible through his carrier. Those three persons were a residence pastor where the accused worships, the translator between the court and the accused, and my humble self. Prior to this statement, an African was accused of a crime and had been sent to court for a hearing. The accused is a man I knew few years ago to be very responsible, God-fearing and hard working. Since he came to my city and introduced himself to me, I tried taking him to different companies and Ministry of Works to see if he could continue with what he'd leaned while he was still in his home country. When that did not workout due to several reasons, he decided to settle for a manual job. While he tried to work to survive, an old issue came up and he was accused of a crime he committed when he first came to Germany. On the day of the court hearing, I went to court as his friend, an African leader and a cofounder of the African Immigrant Integration Centre (A.I.I.C.) Germany. His residence pastor also went with me and the translator, who happens to be a black man. While I tried to talk the prosecutor into tampering justice with mercy on behalf of the accused, he told me that an African had gotten a prison sentence of three and a half years three days earlier in their court. Two days earlier, another was given a jail sentence of two and a half years. While I tried to concentrate on the case at hand, he reminded me that another one may be sentenced the next day, as the court hearing had already been scheduled.

That prosecutor began to see almost every black man as criminal, as he only sees suspected criminals in his courtroom. I tried to make him see the good side of Blackman by letting him know that sending them to jail was not a healthy solution. The root of different crimes must first be addressed, as one problem could lead to another. I also tried to let him know that black people are not criminal-minded as he thought, but I later felt that we could not solve the problem in that court yard. I told him that I need to engage him in a project, not only for him to know black men better but also to check into and fix those things that drives black men to lives of crime. After all the consideration, the accused was given a prison sentence of a few years.

I suddenly turned into a social and political consultant, having found myself in an unplanned leadership position. Each day I wake up, I thank God and ask him for a new strength to face that which is unseen and unknown.

I almost became afraid too, but I just said to myself, *You can't be afraid Eddy*. In a leadership position, I couldn't afford to be afraid. That's why I constantly pray to God for a new strength to carry on. I must say that I have enjoyed God's favour in very special ways.

These words freedom, love, affection, dating, quality, and teenage have become strange and foreign to many people. Some left their homes as a result of political instability, others as a result of economic insecurity, religious values, and many other reasons. Whatsoever the reasons may be, one hopes for a better life in that unknown paradise.

I watched a family friend's children get up several nights to peep through the window to see if police had come to carry them away. There was then so much tension. It meant waking up and being alert at the sound of every passing vehicle. Their asylum case was rejected, and their case file was closed by the authorities. Their three monthly residence permit was withdrawn and replaced with *Duldung* meaning ready to be deported at any time, even though some of the kids were born here. The fear, frustration, and depression the kids went through at that time is unimaginable.

I had much pains in silence at that time over their situation. But I could only spend time with them since that was the most I could do for them.

Some jumped out the window, permanently breaking their legs in fear of police control. Some parents spent nights outside, leaving their children alone in the night so as not to be taken unaware for deportation. Their believe was that the authorities cannot deport kids alone without their parents, and even if they did, some parents are ready to continue running from where ever they may be.

One has to ask where and what is the value of life in the midst of confusion and constant fear?

Many families have been torn apart in the name of paper, loss of value, loss of culture loss of dignity, pride and quality.

Many are moved from their mansions in their home cities to remote villages, having to walk miles to get to the city, turning some of us to an unplanned taxi services.

One is expected to feed on European food since one cannot afford the African food. Some have to get a doctor's report in order to change diet; you don't just have a choice here! Some kids sometimes turn against their parents for bringing them into such a fearful environment.

Siblings deny knowing each other for the sake of staying. Parents sometimes deny their children in order to stay. Husbands deny their wives and wives vice-versa. It's a total confusion for most foreigners.

An African pastor friend who travelled recently to Africa declared upon his return that each time the airplane landed in Africa and the doors opened, he felt as if a heavy load had been lifted off his shoulder. How happy he felt to be back home!

But as long as you stay home, be sure your letters are

being pilled up, waiting for your return as writing and documentary remains a great part of German world.

A 33- year old Ethiopian friend who had been living in Germany for twenty-one years, married to a Yugoslavian woman with two kids, recently exclaimed that he no longer saw brighter future in Europe. He's been working with the German railway as an unskilled worker for some thirteen years, but his salary was barely enough to care for his family. He's just a normal worker who invests most of his time at his work and maintains his monthly bank over draft. There is no fun; he can't afford to travel outside Germany with his family for holiday, let alone think of owning a house. He's planning to make his way to Australia, where he believes it will be better.

"Es ist ein Kreislauf hier. Ich komme nicht vorwärts" he said. *It's a circle here; I can't move further.* I advised him not to leave his family behind, if he must leave.

I was told a story of a Ghanaian who recently collapsed and died at Heathrow_Airport in London, England. It turned out that the man was hypertensive. He had lived in London several years, working too many jobs and not getting enough rest. He barely had time to get some proper medical treatment. He planned his first visit to his home country, but it was too late. While alive, he'd shared an apartment with a friend in order to save money; he worked eighteen to twenty hours daily; he had no car or social life; even going to church on Sundays was a problem because he worked on Sundays as well. As an unskilled worker, he had to work more hours in order to save enough money, after paying his bills for his trip. He worked himself to death saving all that money for nothing. He was supposed to control and treat his blood pressure, but he was too busy working to make more money. Plenty of people hardly have time for medical care because of the several manual jobs they do.

I have some friends in London who know nothing else but work. Some will start their first jobs as early as 5 a. m., finishing at 2 p.m. Then they will start another at 3.30 p.m. and finish at 8 p.m. only to rush home for the last part that starts at 11p.m. and finally closes at 4 a.m. in the morning. All these jobs are in different places. Life is not easy even for indigenes, let alone for foreigners.

The situation for many in Europe is like people aboard an airplane and the pilot suddenly announcing a state of emergency while in the air. He tries everything to land, but he can't - nor can he continue to stay in the air. Imagine the level of fear and panic that would engulf the passengers in the air. That is the best way to describe the situation here. Many people are locked up in their own worlds, pretending that all is fine, even when everything is wrong.

It's sometimes said that Germans don't want you to live and won't allow you to die. You're left hanging in the air!

What is applicable to one person is applicable to most.

Some people even have to be in school forever since they can't get a job after completing their studies. If you're granted a student visa to study in Germany, after studying, you must get a job in the field of your study to stay. If you can't get a job, which is likely since there is high level of unemployment, you marry a German citizen, have a baby, or go to school forever. There is simply no short-cut here. It's a terrible life system.

I do know that some post graduates would like to go back home after their studies, to give back that which they have acquired. This idea of post graduates going back home, or wishing to go back home, I find healthy.

But the situation down home has made even the intellectuals do all it takes to remain in Europe after their studies. What a pity to the African society which has refused to free his people from this modern slavery. Nevertheless, going back home or staying behind remains a personal decision.

Chapter 6

Crime

The black man I know may easily be corrupted but as I said before, he is not crime-minded. He has the fear of God and believes in heaven. Many have dignity, honour and respect and would not want to do away with these principles because of crime. Based on these principles, an average black man who also fears God will try to stay away from all types of crime.

But as time went on, the German police and even some lawyers could describe a black man as possessing lots of criminal energy.

There is a saying that an idle mind is a devil's workshop, and when a man is idle without a job, frustration and hopelessness tend to set-in.

Many came in search of greener pastures and were

shocked to find out that one could make it faster down home than in Europe.

If you're locked up in a room as without future plan, with every kind of movement restricted like a child in a school dormitory, one may be tempted to do black job, but if one is caught doing any form of black job, it might land one in jail. Even if one is in Europe for political reasons, one's life is supposed to continue, but it has proven very difficult. Sometimes one gets more frustrated than ever before.

People are indirectly encouraged to be lazy because one's daily business has been reduced to mere food collection from the shop with one's *schein*.

Given such a situation, one's daily routine becomes limited to cooking, gossiping, and drinking. Consequentially, many will become drunks, their physical and intellectual energy will gradually deteriorate, and evil thoughts will finally set in.

When a black man transforms his physical and intellectual energy into crime, it becomes too devastating for that society. *Man must survive* becomes the language of the day.

By not keeping people busy in one way or another, the government of Germany is not making the situation easier. Instead, one is encouraged to remain at home doing nothing.

Frustration in the environment has made some crimes to become a normal way of living for some people.

Again, most Africans never saw or came in contact with drugs like cocaine, heroin, and even marijuana while in Africa. But don't ask me how it is today in Europe.

I'll never forget when an acquaintance of mine once said that anyone who makes his money on the street must surely pay one day. He believes that he will go to jail one day as long as he remains on the street. But he seems not to have a choice. What a life!

Some survive only through shoplifting. Going to and from jail becomes common for many. Not knowing the hardship people go through in Europe, people at home don't make things easier with their constant calls and demands.

The new trends of living have kept most of our people languishing in jail. I visited someone in jail who would want the authorities to take all the money he made on the street if they would only let him go free. But in Germany, it's not like that. One must be made to serve a prison term if one is caught committing a crime, especially in the case of hard drugs.

Today, most black men are being seen as criminals in the streets of Germany, giving us a new struggle to free ourselves from such social stigma.

Chapter 7

Marriage and Kids

I wouldn't know how bad it was in the days of Sodom and Gomorrah that it made God to destroy the land, but what I see in Germany today, is heart-rending! Obtaining a residence permit in Germany is not press the button and you are there. It requires formidable and demanding efforts. And the saddest thing about it is that one is left with only one choice to make, and that is to play the game according to the rule: since most asylum cases are never granted, marry if you want to stay in Germany. Failure to do so is an indication that one is prepared to face deportation.

The one and only way by which one can prevent deportation has obviously made marriage between German nationals and foreigners lose its value. Specifically, marriage has become a necessity to foreigners. They jump into it and jump out of it as easily as that. Marriage that was ordained by Jehovah

God becomes a shortcut to get there. People rush to disco clubs in search of women to marry; among them are even those who never visited any disco club before. Everything on skirt weather drunk or junkie becomes very interesting as long as German paper could come out there. The authorities will even tell you to marry if you want to stay here!

That reminds me of a friend who one night went with me to a disco club, a popular place to meet women. While we waited at the bus station, we saw a dirty-looking German girl. She looked drunk and was smelling strongly of alcohol. She begged us to give her some coins. My friend said to me, "This could be our luck!" I asked him what he meant by that? He said instead of proceeding to the disco, we could just take the girl home and wash her up. "After all, it's women we were looking for. Who knows? Paper might come out of it", he added. Well I told him that that kind of girl couldn't be my luck. I couldn't imagine having anything to do with such a drunk. Eventually, he decided to take the girl home with him. He called a taxi with the little money he had and did just that. He cleaned her up that night, and the next day, the girl regained her senses and almost made a hell of problem trying to be sure she was not mishandled by my friend.

Thank God the issue didn't go further and the girl went her way. All of this happened in the name of paper.

I'm not trying to paint myself white but I must say that I believe in marriage before sex. My first relationship here in Germany was with a young girl I met in the church. But one of the reasons she broke up with me was because I refused to sleep with her. As a newcomer, I wanted to adhere to my principles, culture and Christian beliefs, but my close friends and some advisers would tell me that such a strategy was never the right way to handle a German woman. They insisted that they were talking from experience. "A German woman needs sex" they would tell me. That relationship winded up after a while since she could really not get anything from me.

I remember one of the girls I later dated. I didn't really know where she came from, but later I discovered that she is connected to Russia. She had told me she was going on holiday to Tunisia. I kept battling within my mind: *A girl who could go on holiday outside Germany must have paper, but what kind of paper?* I asked myself that question because there are different kinds and levels of papers. Did she have a German paper or not? Sometimes I tried checking her wallet and handbag to see her identity card or passport. Asking her if she had a German passport also would have been difficult since she wouldn't understand that. Then I met her mother sometime and found out she was a Russian. So I got more confused because I felt I had no time to waste. In fact the relationship ended since it wasn't certain if she had a German passport or not, even though she was nice.

One has no time to truly get to know a partner that he will spend the rest of his life with. After two weeks of meeting one girl, I proposed marriage to her. She was so shocked, but I told her that I had no time to waste on any girl. I warned her never to call me again until she decided to marry me. She cried. After some weeks, my telephone rang and there she was. I remember asking her if she had decided to marry me now. She said, "Can't you even say hello to me?" I told her I'd said hello to her, and I asked her if she'd decided. She said yes. But we didn't get married.

Marriage, which is one of the greatest things that can happen to mankind has become a cross over in Europe. A young man took a very old woman, old enough to be his grandmother to register to marry. In fact he even had to help the old woman walk. As they got to the registry, their application for a marriage licence was initially turned down because of the wide age difference between them, but after considering the fact that the law says nothing against that, they got married and the guy carried his granny-wife home. There are instances of people talking to some classes of people they would under no circumstances say hello to on the way, if not for Christ. Some people marry with the hope that their partners die soon so that their lives might begin. The plan and hope of many, for that great day when they will be joined together in holy matrimony suddenly turns to a mere dream. Many date and marry people old enough to be their parents. Others would rather never be seen anywhere with their partners; they are simply waiting for their war to be over. They're not proud of what they did but they felt they had no choice.

Some who were even married at home before they travelled, abandoned their wives and children, denying them their marital and parental rites in order to marry in Europe- all in the name of paper.

Since emancipation came to Europe, some German women have begun to consider the ideal way by which a woman should live as old-fashioned.

I remember one old German woman who was once my landlady and a member of our parish. She took special interest in me and treated me like a son. She told me a little story of her olden days, when great family values existed in Germany. She told me of her late parents, how harmoniously they lived until they died.

She even talked about her husband, who took ill and died not long before that. How happy they were as a family while he lived, and how her motherly role was graciously appreciated. She had six children with her husband and they happily raised them together. She was a sales woman who was content to take on a motherly role while her husband worked for Volkswagen as an engineer. She would tell me. "Please be careful of today's German women. They are highly emancipated." I would sometimes respond by saying "Oma, as I call her, "all German women are not the same. She would respond that she agreed, but she also pointed out that the rate of divorce was rising and that the kinds of women she saw these days were widely different from what she knew in her days. They all want to be free, independent, and masters of their own.

I recall telling the mother of my first son years ago, while we lived together, that if she ever went through my personal belongings or tried to lock me out- no matter what the reason may be, it would mark the end of our relationship. They are fond of locking their men outside and trying to apologise the next day.

If a German woman locks her husband out or calls the police on him, no court will jail her for it. In fact, police will even escort the man out of the house and possibly forbid him from coming home without the woman's consent. A European woman may love you with all her heart, but be strong and ready to accept it, if her love expires. This will be independent of whether kids are involved or not.

Society has given them so much power and protection which some of them sometimes overuse. Once a German woman decides to leave her husband, especially when little kids are involved and the man is working, the council will support her by offering her an apartment and paying her some social welfare, so she has no time to think about mending her relationship. She has the money, and the state is on her side, so what's the problem? Shortly afterwards, the man's salary will be calculated to see if he is in a position to pay the woman some money every month for her upkeep. While there are always exceptions to every classification, in this case, there are few. The situation reflects the proverb about German women being like German weather- they can change at anytime. And some German women are even proud of that saying.

What importance do you attach to marriage? What value do you attach to life? What culture do you preach? Not to sound racist, but the European way of life is something that you can't just change.

African husbands are often neglected in making important decisions, as it is often believed that they know nothing or do not understand the language. I remember almost suing some medical doctors who operated on my boy to court. I carefully watched the incident occur and reoccur. Several times I visited the doctor with my ex-wife and my boy. The doctors didn't even notice that I was present. I was completely neglected, as if I were not there. I watched it happen several times before I complained to my boy's mum, but kept such incidence for record purposes. In Germany, kids are expected to report to the doctor for every little thing.

All the same, a serious incident happened when I was supposed to make a business trip to Munich. My boy was to be operated upon, so I had to cancel my journey in order to stay with them and be part of the signatory. When we arrived at the hospital, a doctor came with his team, held out his hand to the mother of my son, and started talking to her about the operation. I listened carefully to the discussions. I understood even better than she did, having studied anatomy and psychology at the university. But I was not even noticed, nor greeted, let alone asked to sign, the operation warrant. When she was given the operation warrant to sign. I almost exploded. I allowed them to finish the operation, which went successfully, before addressing that issue at that hospital. When they heard me speak German after introducing myself, the whole team was shocked because if that operation had not been successful, they would have known that I know a little of that which they know in the medical field and probably more in the insurance industry because I did not sign for that operation to be carried out as the father, even though I was there.

I have always loved children, but I never actually planned to have a child of my own. However, when my boy was born, I discovered the joy of having a child. In fact I always feel like exploding with happiness each time I think of my boy. I love him so much!

The law of the land, which was supposed to be healthy, has even made it sometimes unhealthy for many who still have real value for life. It was said that if you have a child with a German citizen, you may be permitted to stay in Germany, for the sake of the child. Therefore, men started making kids as long as women were ready to carry babies, and women started hanging out with any men bearing German citizenship as long as such men were ready to get them pregnant. Singles mothers everywhere and don't bother asking some of them the where about of their men because you never can find them.

The situation has made people lose the real value for kids and marriage. It serves them as a shortcut in achieving their objective, which is a German paper or citizenship. For heaven's sake, where are we heading?

What has our world turned to? In a world where women and police rule, one can imagine the result such a society could produce. Some women misuse their legal power in Europe by making their male partners, who have little or no choice, be like slaves. Some lock their men out in the night for funny reasons, irrespective of whether children are involved or not.

Some German women fall in love with men who

seemingly have no future with them. They go out with such men just for sexual reasons alone. Enjoy it while it lasts, they say, thus treating love, marriage, relationships, partnerships and dating as a pure game. May God forgive us all! Amen.

Chapter 8

The Worth of Man

Some years ago, I was at work in Düsseldorf, one of the biggest cities in Germany, when a phone call came in from Hamburg, asking me to please do all I could to identify and clear up a death issue concerning a Nigerian involved in an accident on Highway number 7.

I had to start going into details with the police station and hospital authorities. First was to help establish his identity since he was staying in Germany as a Sudanese citizen. I tried to find out the cause of his death and eventually discovered that it was partially caused by his possessing a wrong identity. I never knew him prior to that, but I had to get involved when others may have lacked courage.

Even after death, do not think the war is over here. It might become the beginning of a new chapter, as it almost was in the case of that young man. He had travelled in a car with two others whose identities were probably for one reason or another, in question. It was winter and snowing. He was in the backseat alone. As their vehicle lost control, and began to tumble, he fell off from the back screen since he was not wearing the safety belt. He landed on his chest on the highway, as reported by the police officer in charge.

The highway police came to the scene of the accident and rushed him to the hospital. After two days in the hospital without genuine identity, he died. And the others who were involved in the accident went on the run. I could neither question the police nor the hospital authorities regarding the kind of treatment he received because the issue became even more complicated in the case of death. I identified him as a Nigerian with the help of the Nigerian embassy, and not the Sudanese. I got some documents from the Nigeria embassy and contacted his people in Nigeria with the help of some Hamburg people who brought me onto the scene. I got his people an invitation letter with the help of the police officer in charge of the matter.

A complete photo documentary was made and delivered to his people, who never initially believed their son died in a car crash. It took a considerable length of time before I could get all the necessary papers ready to transport his remains back home to his wife and family.

The story became even more tragic when his people came to me from Nigeria, bringing his wedding photographs of his beautiful young wife. I cried because of such a great loss. After the corpse was transported home, I was faced with another issue: his hospital bills and the social/welfare money spent on him while he was still alive, which amounted to several thousands of euro. Only God knows how I survived that. This is just to let you know that even after death, it's possibly not over. That was how that young huge looking man's journey ended. He might have promised his wife that he'd make it in a short while and come back home. As an African leader, a social activist, a professional insurance man, and a financial consultant, I've heard numerous pathetic stories of ugly experiences from people across Germany.

I visited one of my clients in one of the big cities in Germany. And in the course of our discussion, he showed me a picture of his daughter, who lives with her German mother, from whom he was divorced. Tears began streaming down his face as he showed me the picture of his daughter. I asked him her name, but he kept shedding tears. I asked him to stop crying and tell me the name of his daughter. He wiped his tears and said her name was "Ije-ego," meaning "because of money." He had travelled to Germany several years before and gotten married like many others would do without choice.

After his daughter was born, he tried to save his trouble-filled marriage. His ex-wife finally asked him to leave the house, while his daughter remained with her. His ex-wife fought hard to retain custody of their daughter and she got it. It wasn't his plan to marry and leave his children somewhere. I tried to encourage him not to lose faith in his child, no matter the circumstances.

My company sent me for a financial consultation to someplace in Nordrhein-Westfalen, one of the biggest states in Germany. It was a predominantly African group. After my consultations, several professional questions were entertained, after which one of the oldest among them wanted to talk to me privately. I listened as he poured out his heart to me in the way a child would. He was about 60 years old, if I'm not mistaken, and he said he had just been released from jail.

He had a German wife and children who had left him in his old age. He had declared a much younger age to the authorities when he came to Germany decades earlier, as he was wrongly advised by some unprofessional advisers. He had no regular job and lived in a single room. His kids couldn't care less about him, and even at his age, he was still doing manual jobs here and there. But unfortunately, he couldn't retire because of his young declared age. Even when he retired, his gratuity would not feed him, let alone pay his rent since he never had a professional job. He was highly frustrated and could only think of committing crimes, even at his age. Going home was already a nightmare for him. One of his greatest wishes was to visit home, but how? But it wasn't that paper was the issue. He couldn't afford a plane ticket with his meagre income. I almost left the job I'd gone to do and started thinking of what to do for that elderly man. I remember telling him not to commit suicide while I thought of a way to do something for him. Every one you encounter across the way has his own story.

Frustration in Europe can sometime make one abandon his loved ones.

An acquaintance of mine who lives in East Germany left his people in Africa so worried and upset for over ten years they almost believed he was dead. He came to Germany more than fifteen years earlier. He'd maintained contact with his people in the beginning, hoping that things would get better soon. But as the wind of Germany blew him, he dropped contact with his people in Africa for more than ten years, leaving his entire family terribly worried.

His people in Africa made several efforts to determine whether he was still alive, but all to no avail until his family made a loud cry to one of his countrymen who also lives in Germany. His family went to his countryman's house as he visited home. His countryman promised his people in Africa that he was going to do everything possible to find him. When he returned to Germany, he started his search mission to look for our African brother. In fact, to see him, touch him, make photograph with him and let him also talk to his people in Africa who do no longer know what to believe. His countryman told me this when he first met me to help him look for our African brother. When I heard about the issue, I went into action immediately. A week later, I was able to draw the African brother to my office from where he lived hundreds of kilometres away. A reunion was celebrated and I thanked all those who aided in that mission, especially his countryman who brought me into the scene. I partly understand that African brother's situation considering the extent of pressure he has to battle with in Germany. It wasn't his plan to abandon his people. His people in Africa could not contain their joy on that day; even as they announced how only hearing his voice alone would increase their life spans.

Some people came to Europe by air, some by sea, some by land, and many even walked several miles across the desert to get there. And some people are still hanging somewhere on the way, while many others felled on the roadside and never made it after all. But the lingering question is who will be brave enough to confront the truth and present the situation exactly the way it is? There are lies and fear everywhere. People even lie to themselves. Each person is carrying his or her own mountain of problems but pretending that all is well. What a pity! What a world!

I was once called to supervise one of the refugee homes popularly known as an asylum house in Vellmar, which is in my state. What I saw there was unbelievable how people could live in such a disgusting environment in Germany. There were cockroaches everywhere as well as damaged cooking utensils and water closets with a very bad main entrance. I made a photographic documentary of the place and immediately went into discussion with the caretaker of the place, who responded that he could do little or nothing about the situation. He later directed me to a higher authority, someone responsible for the people leaving there. I went to the authority in charge and lodged a complaint concerning the health situation in that place.

I insisted that such a place could not be suitable for human beings. We discussed whether to renovate or close down the place. The authority in charge gave me an appointment for two weeks later, which I kept. The authority told me an eventual misunderstanding arose between the social authorities and the real owner of the house since the house was rented from a private owner. To make a long story short the place was then closed down shortly afterwards and the people living there were happy and thankful to God.

Some people had been brave to report the issue to me, and I used courage from God to follow up on the issue just as I had with many other related issues.

The world around us here in Europe has brought more confusion than solutions. The exodus of those already here in Europe is now even worse than those in Africa. People are confused; they don't know a way out of the situation. They move from one country to another.

Before now, people had moved from England to Germany, but today it's all roads from Germany to London, Ireland, Canada, the United States, and even as far as Australia. Many people leave their wives and kids behind, adding to the ones some already left in Africa to join still another unknown world.

One of my homeboys has gradually assumed "No Land" as a name. He always say, "No father, no mother, no family, and no land." He's been in Europe for eighteen years and in Germany for twelve. He told me how he had hidden himself somewhere under a ship from one of the African countries in other to make his way to Europe. He has been taken to most African embassies in Berlin for identification, but he cannot be properly identified. So when I sometimes call him homeboy, he will respond, "No name, no family, and no land." It's a very serious issue for someone who spent eighteen years in Europe.

It's true that since the unification of Germany, the introduction of the euro, and the recent reunification of Europe, life in Europe, especially in Germany, where I live, has become tougher than it formerly was. I had friends who left Germany for London and came back shortly afterwards.

Others left and remained where they went. But who says it's better somewhere else? And how long shall we continue to be a boy in a new world. It's all about confusion and indecision, but remember that the purpose of every journey must be well defined.

Chapter 9

Discrimination

And who says it's over when the so-called paper is obtained? That's just the end of one phase and the beginning of the real war. Some years ago, I applied for a job with a company that needed a German citizen. I told them I have the status of a German citizenship. I told them I have the status of a German citizenship. They told me, "Sorry, but we need a German." This is not a new issue, even though discrimination is against the German law.

I took some time visiting some nightclubs in my city after several complaints from blacks and other foreigners who were denied entry to some clubs. In other to confirm those complaints, I visited about six clubs in one night and got the shock of my life that even in disco clubs, where people relax after a week of hard work on the job, it is becoming a big problem in our society. Most foreigners won't be allowed entry. To my surprise, I managed to enter three clubs, but in the other three, I was turned down. I tried to find out why I wasn't allowed to enter, and they gave me no tangible reasons.

One of the bouncers from one of the clubs shocked me by telling me in my face that the club owner wanted only Germans to come into his disco club. He added that he might lose his job if I stayed longer outside unless I was ready to give him a job. "Sorry" he said. I didn't need to show him that I was carrying a German passport because it wouldn't make any difference to him. It was then that I knew what had been going on in the clubs.

One of my Eritrean friends told me how he was disgraced before his wife in one of the disco clubs in the city where I live. He had had some misunderstanding with his wife at home for some time. He lost his temper in the house and quarrelled over every little thing; it was no longer an enjoyable atmosphere for their two little kids.

His mother-in-law then asked them to go out one evening together, while she took care of the kids to see if they could enjoy themselves and get to understand each other again. My friend welcomed the offer and decided to take his white wife out to one of the disco clubs. He said he hadn't been to a club for a long time.

When they got to the club, they left the car together and my friend forgot something in the car and had to rush back out while his wife had entered and waited by the door. He quickly returned to his wife, who was still waiting for him. His day, which had already been bad, became worse when he was refused entry to the club. He tried asking why but got no reasonable answer. His wife who was still by the door, told them that the guy in question was her husband, and one of the bouncers asked her what she was even doing with that guy. She left the club with her husband her eyes filled with tears. If a German want to go out, he says to himself, *where do I party tonight?* He has options. However, when a black man wants to go out, he says to himself, *Where will I be allowed in tonight?* What a pity!

Thank God at least for the freedom that exists in the church, the house of God.

In my city, about thirty policemen recently ransacked with dogs, the car shop belonging to one of my friend. He's been dealing with vehicles for more than fifteen years now and has contacts almost worldwide.

It was alleged that he had 144,000 euros transferred into his account from different places. His bank had informed the police, and the police got a search warrant from the state justice to ransack his place of business and his home. This is a businessman who could control millions of euros.

He had several vehicles – cars, trucks, and more- for sale in his garage, and was being questioned about 144.000euros. That's the place we are. It takes a whole lot to come up here. You're not allowed to rest; it doesn't matter how clean you try to be.

I would still encourage those already here not to give up the fight, especially those with kids. It will take a long fight to be part of this world.

Don't allow depression to overtake you. Keep your head up!

We all experience constant pressure and panic on a daily basis. Don't give up! We may not really fit into the African system again, having lived so long here and having established ourselves in one way or another. But at the same time, our African leaders and brothers should try to save us the unnecessary war of trying to belong to a foreign world. Please save the African world and spare us the trauma we undergo daily in foreign lands.

I do hear some people say, "if you leave police alone, police will live you alone." No! Not in the case of Germany. It's sometimes worse when one wants to become somebody here. One begins to ask himself several questions: Where do we truly belong? Where is life worth living? What is the value of life? But is migration the solution? I doubt.

A boy whose residence permit was withdrawn and was given two weeks to leave Germany, having been rejected asylum after his short stay, had an appointment with me to take him to a lawyer. When he got to my city, we were almost running out of time, so he had to make several calls on the way, and I told him over the phone how to get to our meeting point. As soon as I picked him up, several policemen rounded us up.

They had their vehicles in the front and the other in the back, leaving us in the middle. As they rushed us like criminals, I stepped out of the car and asked them what the issue was. They asked the boy to step out of the car and started with what they called personal control of his papers. When the policemen saw that he has only two weeks in his paper to stay in Germany, after which he must leave, they said we could go now. Well I insisted on knowing why they rushed us the way they did. They told me that they saw the boy I picked up making several calls with a mobile telephone along the way.

So they wanted to know who he was and what he did. "So does that mean a black man cannot make calls along the way? I asked them. They said that in this case, they saw him making longer calls. Since we were already running out of time, we decided to leave so as not to waste more time.

I was once involved in an accident when my traffic right was obstructed by another driver. A Russian ran into my car, saying he had been distracted by his girlfriend. I called the police. When they came, they started searching me all over as a criminal would be searched, leaving the Russian guy, who was at fault, standing aside, even though I had vehicle papers and my driving licence. I have not stayed up to two years in Germany then. The father of my then German girlfriend later went to police station with me to discuss the intimidating attitude with the police in charge. I was quite inexperienced and afraid then. These ugly treatments one encounters daily in Europe could compel one to become hot-tempered. But a problem recognised is half-solved, so by God's grace, I wouldn't be hot-tempered myself. After all, Europeans didn't force anyone to come to Europe.

Discrimination is still eating deep in the minds of several Germans and even the authorities.

A Kenyan practicing medical doctor's friend who had lived in Germany for thirty-five years complained how he must work harder among his colleagues to be recognised and commended. He is always punctual, takes little or no sick leave, and works even when his colleagues smoke. He often puts in overtime even when he is not in the mood. "It's not normal," he said. He' has to work like a horse daily. Well, you must not make it double when and where it has to be single to please anyone and probably get sick. Just because it's not our world, and one would take much longer time to make it ours.

An Afghanistan medical doctor, who is also a friend of mine and who schooled with me here some time ago, got so frustrated here that he might have given up living if not for his two lovely kids and wife he'd brought with him. He said he'd left Afghanistan some years ago for political reasons. Back home in Afghanistan, he had worked in a university teaching hospital and run a day clinic too. Since he came to Germany, he could not even get the opportunity to serve as a nurse, let alone assist a doctor. When I schooled with him, he had struggled to do his practical in a hospital. He got a position assisting a doctor in a hospital but was asked to produce 1,001 papers to prove his medical knowledge. During that practice, he submitted all his credentials and answered all the necessary question that arose, but he was still not allowed to practice anywhere in Germany. Even when his countryman who runs a clinic here tried helping him, perhaps to assist him in his clinic, he was still not given the permission to practice here as a medical doctor.

While in school, we all respected him and called him doctor because it's not easy to be one. He had thought the whole class including the lecturer in the class each time a medical topic arose. I enjoyed being with him and also shared his agony.

The only African restaurant in my city was stormed some years ago, by more than ten policemen, for no good reason. Police said that the neighbours complained that there were blacks coming in and out, also saying that the place was noisy. People were seated and eating when they rushed in. I confronted them with several questions, which got them pointing guns at me, though I knew they were not going to shoot. I was furious that day and went to a radio station with a colleague of mine for a broadcast concerning that ugly control.

To that effect, my friends and I later organised a demonstration with some dedicated Africans. The police president and his colleagues had invited my friend and me to see if we could call off the planned demonstration, but we wanted to create some awareness in the city, and the demonstration was successful. But the number of customers dropped drastically, and the

African restaurant died because most blacks are still afraid and cannot stand such controls and intimidation. It was a big loss and regret to all Africans in my city.

The question of discrimination cannot be over emphasised, but thank God for some few dedicated German Christians and politicians who see black, yellow, green, and other white foreigners as brothers.

Chapter 10

The Real Man

Some years ago, a classmate of mine from Nigeria, pressured me hard, waiting to come over to Germany. He was still serving in one of the American oil servicing companies in Nigeria, but he suddenly became desperate to leave. I told him the truth about it here in Germany, telling him how frustrated he would be if he made the journey to Germany.

At first, he thought I was not ready to help him, especially when I brought a used Mercedes Benz car home.

He became sceptical about staying in Nigeria, and he finally decided that if the company he served did not retain him, he would definitely leave the country. Well, I remember wishing and praying that he was retained so he would forget the issue of coming to Germany.

If he had come here then, believe me, it could have been a suicidal mission for him because he's not even that strong, and his carrier and profession would have been a forgotten issue. As God would have it, he was retained as a drilling engineer in his company, and the issue of coming to Germany was dropped. Today he is a professional who tours around the world without fear.

He was recently posted to the USA by his company. He is happily married with two kids.

It is a rare instance when someone tells another the truth about staying in Europe, and the person welcomes that truth with joy and understanding. He's a great friend, and I'm proud of him.

The real man will tell his friend the truth, and a real man should welcome such truth. It's not about travelling, but in what condition you would want to travel.

I had an opportunity to dine with President Obasanjo on one of his visits to Germany some time ago. I asked His Excellency what he thought about the issue of our people going back home. Baba, as he was popularly called, responded that home was good, but one must plan and think very well before going home. Home is good! Quit encouraging. But the idea of thinking and planning very well before going home wasn't good enough.

I expected African leaders with sound minds to encourage their people to come back home, especially ones with interest.

Numerous people living at home are better off than many leaving anywhere abroad. People lacked the real truth. Tell yourself the truth which will help convince others too. Stop deceiving yourself; come out with your problems and ask for help.

A 35-years-old Ethiopian friend who recently went back to Ethiopia has this to say. He had lived in Germany for more than eighteen years, learnt electrical and had worked in a private company in Germany for over fifteen years. He has a 9-year-old boy with a German woman, and she would not let him have custody of the boy. He said has lost the joy of living. He could no longer laugh, had constant psychological pains, and frowned unnecessarily at people.

He said he knew the cause his problem because a friend of his had a similar problem and was put on antidepressants. But he refused to give in. He stopped working. His pension and gratuity amounted to 450 euros monthly. After his pension issue was cleared, he decided to go back to Ethiopia.

He called my office after he arrived in Ethiopia, while I was with the friend who took him to the airport, to tell me how happy he felt leaving Germany. At Frankfurt Airport, he wept, as he was going to miss some friends. But back home, he could laugh again. He found joy and meaning in life again. Depression and psychological pains were gone and he felt great going back to his world. With great joy and satisfaction, he has started practicing the modern electrical technology that he had acquired while he was still in Germany.

Several people have been placed on antidepressants here because they are stressed out. Such drugs are prescribed easily, but whether they produce any good results, is another thing. Better to stay away from them, as they don't provide any lasting solution.

I've tried to categorise people into three classes in order to find out why one has to travel. The first class of people are mainly expatriates, depending on their field of specialisation-for instance diplomats, special agents, NGOs, missionaries, family reunion/marriage, businessmen (who of course, should go back after their business trips are over), and students. The lives of these ones can only continue without necessarily being taken backward. The second class represents the political refugees, who have no choice. While the third class represents the taut who are hopeless, homeless, futureless, and highly destabilised. This class could be thrown out of the country, who knows, they might become something or somebody someday. Find out for yourself which classes you belong to.

A man from Nigeria whom I don't even know, recently called my phone and asked to speak to his son. He introduced himself and said the name of his son, who was supposed to be leaving in Germany. I didn't recognise his son's name. He agreed we had never met before, and that his son had given him my number some years ago. I asked him what he wanted from me, and he asked me to please bring his son back home. I asked what he meant by that. He said he heard I'm a leader in Germany and a friend to his son. He told me that he had not heard from his son for several months, and that he and his wife were worried. His son had left home several years earlier and never returned since then. Both parents had tried to talk their son into coming back home at least to see him but without success. Well I promised to help him look for his son having felt his agony through that telephone discussion, and I'm still trying to find out who bears the name he mentioned. That was that young man's journey. Only God knows what he bears as name and what nationality he declared. The man pleaded so much with me to help get his son back home otherwise he would go to German Embassy in Nigeria to find out more about his son.

I was told the story of a friend who lives in Essen, Germany. He had lived in Germany for a rather long time, worked several years, and later started a business importing and exporting spare motor spare parts with a bank loan. He bought some old cars, dismantled them, and sent them to Nigeria, as many have been doing. After a while, his elder brother, who was a pastor at home in Nigeria, started pressuring him, saying that he would like to come to Germany.

My friend in Germany tried to explain to his elder brother in Nigeria that life was not easy here, as he thought. But his elder brother insisted and even promised to do any kind of job that might be available. The pastor's decision remained immutable. Eventually, he made it to Germany, his dream land, thinking that his struggle in life was over. While in Germany, his brother, who had helped the pastor come over and was still ready to establish him, took him to Essen Dellwig, where vehicles of all kinds are dismantled and loaded into containers for shipment. When they got there, his brother showed the pastor what to do. The pastor was to pick some vehicles parts together and load them into a container with other younger boys he had been working with. The Pastor asked his brother if picking of parts, loading, and unloading with small boys who talk anyhow was the job he wanted him to do over here? Well, his brother had no other options. In fact, he was even lucky, I would say, to have gotten such a black job so he could get some money without proper documentation.

Unfortunately, the pastor could no longer do the job of loading and unloading containers. He finally decided to leave Germany for good. He saw and made a quicker decision.

One of my favourite stories is that of a woman who took her son to a warrior to help him stop eating sugar. The warrior told the woman and her son to leave and come back in two weeks time. They returned to the warrior after two weeks, and the warrior looked at the boy and said to him. "Stop eating sugar!" The woman asked the warrior why he couldn't say this to her son two weeks earlier. The warrior responded: "Then, I was eating sugar."

The warrior lived by example. Remember, it's your life, and every decision you make about it matters a great deal. The real man will begin with himself, as the warrior did.

I would advise those living in Europe to be honest with themselves and present the situation to those at home exactly as it is. Start with your families and your communities. I've discouraged several relatives and friends who have no good reason to travel to rather stay behind instead, and believe me many of them are happy and thankful today. The resources that one would use to travel to Europe would be more than enough to make one live comfortably in Africa.

But if you have a good and genuine reason to travel, no one says not to do that!

A Libyan client, who is an IT professional, was recently posted to Germany by his company. He left what he came to do in my office and started complaining about Europe. He felt mad about the whole system, his take home pay, taxes, and people's unfriendly attitude towards him- even at his place of work. He felt he couldn't fit in here, and he was already pressing hard to go back home. I told him to take it easy, adding that he is on a professional journey. So what does he expect many others who came ordinarily to do? It is all about personal choice and decision.

The real man will define and redefine the purpose of his journey because when purpose is not known, abuse becomes inevitable. The real man tries to know where he belongs.

For those who are still planning to sell off their lives in order to make it down here, ask your brothers and true friends who are already in Europe to tell you the truth and reality of it all, how they really survive and what they do to survive.

I can hear some readers saying that if it's that bad, why don't you come back home? Yes, I might go back home one day, when my mission is completed Just consider me as a part of a research programme.

The lost ones here also have to be found, accommodated, and integrated including our innocent kids.

And I'm also not suggesting that those already in Europe should begin to rush back home without a plan; nor am I saying that Europe has turned hostile. No! It's just not our world. There are some who can no longer go home, especially those with kids. Those kids are innocent and must not be allowed to go through the trauma we are going through. So those already in Europe have to be brought back to the reality of life by re-educating them in different ways. Many are confused and can no longer direct themselves. Every African has a big role to play in this issue, especially those in leadership positions. Migrating can never be the answer. Let us all save the African world! It is not impossible.

Chapter 11

Time to Rethink

I do not want to emphasise poverty, but some so-called men of God today, especially in Africa, lay so much emphasis on riches, money, and wealth, thereby driving our youths and even adults into believing that poverty is a curse. I believe in poverty as much as I believe in riches.

Even our Lord Jesus Christ demonstrated poverty through his birth in a manger. Yes, he suffered humiliation, died for our sins, and made poor to bring us riches. But what kinds of riches? How do you define riches? What is wealth for you?

Jesus was the poorest, the most humble, a servant of all, and a sacrificial lamb.
He had no servants, yet they called him Master.
He had no degree, yet they called him Teacher.

He had no medicine, yet they called him Healer.
He had no army, yet kings feared him.
He won no military battles, yet he conquered the world.
He committed no crime, yet he was crucified.
He was buried in a tomb, yet he lives today.
He remains the greatest man in history.

What are wealth and riches to you? What is your own definition of wealth? What is your own definition of poverty? Are riches to you all about money?

What is money to you? Is money your own definition of wealth? Is lack of money a definition of poverty to you?

I'm not trying to contradict issues here. One must not be poor or financially handicapped, but I think it's high time our religious leaders redefined poverty, riches, and wealth for a better understanding to the ordinary man.

Politics and politicians have failed us. Must our religious leaders fail us too? They are supposed to be the new hope when politics fail.

Money! Money! Money, is that the real wealth for you? Is that the real treasure for you? Is that the riches that Jesus came to teach? What could you exchange money for?

Jesus is the richest man, our Great Master, the owner of everything and through whom salvation is sure. Jesus is the owner of money, good health, riches, wealth, power, happiness, joy, love, and every good thing.

I believe that a godly, quiet, happy, peaceful, healthy, heavenly, stable home is a wealthy home! That which only Jesus gives is what makes a people and a nation, for instance inner satisfaction, sound mind, and joy. Until we realise these factors, we may never understand where we're going and what we're looking for. These rules apply to both individuals and leaders.

I do know that the issues of corruption and mis-management have been discussed repeatedly in regards to African countries. And some African countries, especially Nigeria, remain among the most corrupt countries in the world. I would want to use this medium, once again to urge our people, and especially our leaders, to think beyond just their families and personal luxuries. And when I say leaders, I do not just mean the presidents and the governors: every level of leadership has a big role to play in this issue. No level of leadership is small or easy!

> **Reject and refuse corruption in its entirety. This will bring us far and reduce the agony our people go through in foreign lands. Every individual has a role to play. Just <u>believe</u>, <u>begin</u> and <u>become</u> it. Wake up and stop dreaming it! It is possible.**

Those who discourage the government from finding a lasting solution to the energy crisis in Nigeria because they want to sell their imported generators, imported gas, and imported oil should rethink. Those who discourage enough water supplies in other to boost their boreholes and water supply trade should rethink.

We need one united country, despite the different languages. Those who separate our country by hiding under the guise of different languages should rethink and remember that a country's national language or languages strengthens and unifies her.

A country like Nigeria could constitutionally strengthen her states government in order to make room for healthy competition in the area of development.

Those who use ordinary sand instead of stone to construct our roads in order to make maximum profit should rethink.

Those who discourage all forms of production activities just to profit their import businesses should rethink. Those who encourage and push their daughters into offering their bodies for money in Europe should rethink and remember that life does not end here. Those who prepare fake travel documents and never travel themselves should rethink.

Those who do cleaning and other manual jobs in Europe in order to survive, and those who indulge in one criminal act or another, in order to make money, only to dress in suits like chief executives when they travel to Africa, thereby driving many others back home into believing that all is well in Europe should rethink and stop deceiving themselves as well as many others.

Those who empty the national coffers and send them overseas, while they still live in the hell of Africa should rethink.

Africans, and specifically Nigerians, are not even asking for much. We only ask for good roads, water, a steady energy supply, medical care, education, and transparency in all walks of life. Why should we depend mostly on import? Why do some people discourage production?

Why do we train production engineers? There are now Indian and Chinese motorcycles everywhere, just to profit some few persons. All these shortsighted strategies can only benefit us in the short run.

What happens tomorrow?

The issue is not coming to Europe or travelling out, but what plans and in what condition would you want to travel? I've seen blacks try to take their lives, an act which is not common in the black race. This is just the beginning of the story, but for everyone, it is time to rethink!

And don't forget that God's time is always the best for us.

About the Author

Eddy K. Duru is a Nigerian of Igbo origin with a German nationality. He schooled in Nigeria and Germany, respectively. He is one of the African leaders in Germany, a permanent member of the Igbo Representative Council, Germany, and a cofounder of the African Immigrant Integration Centre (AIIC), Germany.

He is also a financial consultant, agent and Controller for Ria Money Transfer Kassel: a sales representative for Deutscher Herold Versicherungen: and an insurance expert, IT specialist, and the director of Green Communication and More.

For further information, contact:
Green Communication and More
Hedwigstraße.10-12; (near city point)
34117 Kassel Germany

Voice: 49 561 76690597
Fax: 49 561 76690596
Mobile: +49 162 15 22 508
E-mail eddyherold@yahoo.com
www.greenandmore-kassel.com

www.ingramcontent.com/pod-product-compliance
Lightning Source LLC
Chambersburg PA
CBHW020337290526
45785CB00005B/2055